# THE MOOD BOOK

PHOEBE GLENN

Balboa Press books may be ordered through booksellers or by contacting:

Balboa Press
A Division of Hay House
1663 Liberty Drive
Bloomington, IN 47403
www.balboapress.com
844-682-1282

ISBN: 979-8-7652-5203-1 (sc)
ISBN: 979-8-7652-5081-5 (hc)
ISBN: 979-8-7652-5080-8 (e)

Library of Congress Control Number: 2024908847

Print information available on the last page.

Balboa Press rev. date: 06/18/2024

BALBOA.PRESS
A DIVISION OF HAY HOUSE

# THE MOOD BOOK

The Mood Book is for you to enjoy. It is your tool. A tool that you can use however feels good to you. I have found The Mood Book to be rewarding when reading it at the beginning of my day, when manifesting, as a mood reset, as inspiration, visualization, or merely to add to the aesthetics of my space. Whether having coffee in your favorite chair or wrapping it up as a gift...its flexibility allows inspiration to be mobile. It is the solution for screen-free visual inspiration in our daily lives. Visualizations accompanied by emotions are the most powerful tools we have, and by reading this book I hope to stimulate emotional visualizations for your life. You can choose to use the pictures and words literally as they appear or as a symbol for what you are attracting into your life.

I am so excited about what this book will inspire for you in your life. Happy dreaming!

You are magic,

Phoebe

WWW.ELEVEN22MOOD.COM

# CLEAR YOUR DESK.
# TIE YOUR HAIR UP.
# GRAB A COFFEE.
# AND JUST START.

IMAGINE THE WOMAN YOU WANT TO BE. THINK OF WHAT HER DAILY LIFE, HER HABITS, HER ROUTINES WOULD BE. START SHOWING UP TO THOSE HABITS AND ROUTINES, START BUILDING THEM, STEP BY STEP, AND DAY BY DAY.

-JAMIE VARON

TRY TO SAY NOTHING NEGATIVE
ABOUT ANYBODY FOR THREE DAYS,
FOR FORTY-FIVE DAYS, FOR THREE
MONTHS.

SEE WHAT HAPPENS TO YOUR LIFE.
-YOKO ONO

JUST IN CASE YOU
WERE WONDERING
IT TURNS OUT
BETTER THAN YOU
COULD HAVE EVER
IMAGINED.

THE MAGIC IS

IN

YOU BABY

This is the
beginning of
anything you want.

# GET READY BEAUTIFUL GIRL. IT'S ABOUT TO RAIN MAGIC.

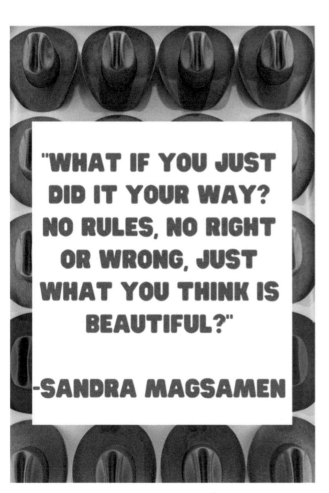

"WHAT IF YOU JUST DID IT YOUR WAY? NO RULES, NO RIGHT OR WRONG, JUST WHAT YOU THINK IS BEAUTIFUL?"

-SANDRA MAGSAMEN

Do not settle for allowing your life to simply be okay. Or fine. Or even just good. Make it extraordinary. Make it thrilling. Make it spectacular. Fill it with excitement and passion, adventures and opportunities. You only get one beautiful life, make it magical and above all else, make it yours.
-Alysha Waghorn

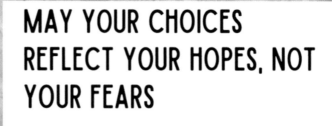

MAY YOUR CHOICES
REFLECT YOUR HOPES, NOT
YOUR FEARS

-NELSON MANDELA

GO TO BED TONIGHT WITH
NOTHING BUT LOVE AND
GRATITUDE IN YOUR HEART.
WHAT IS MEANT TO BE WILL BE.
ENJOY THE PROCESS.

FOLLOWING YOUR BLISS WILL
LEAD YOU TO EVERYTHING
THAT YOU WANT.

-ABRAHAM HICKS

## CHOOSE A THOUGHT

Pretend it's already happened. Get
excited about it.

Watch what happens.
-Abraham Hicks

I WILL NEVER HAVE
THIS VERSION OF
ME AGAIN.
LET ME SLOW
DOWN AND BE WITH
HER.
-RUPI KAUR

YOU ARE CAPABLE OF CREATING
THE LIFE YOU CAN'T STOP
THINKING ABOUT. STOP LIVING IN
YOUR HEAD. IT'S TIME TO MAKE
YOUR DREAMS HAPPEN.

THAT PODCAST? LAUNCH IT.
THAT BLOG? START IT.
THAT BOOK? WRITE IT.
THAT IDEA? FLESH IT OUT.
THAT APP? DEVELOP IT.
THAT GIFT? PUT IT TO USE.
THAT LIFE? LIVE IT.

She is CEO of her own creative company.
She goes from meeting to meeting in the
daytime, client dinners in the evenings,
and travels from coast to coast. She stays
in the finest hotels in the World, is in
Dubai one day, London the next, Tokyo
and NYC before the weekend. She is very
fashionable wears only the best and has a
personal shopper.

-glambarbiesocialite

# SHE BELIEVED SHE COULD, SO SHE DID.

# HAVE A DREAM SO CLEAR IN YOUR MIND THAT YOU HAVE ALREADY ACHIEVED IT.

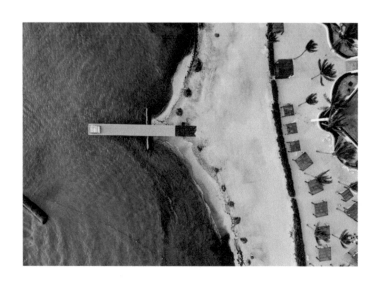

"MAKE A LIST OF POSITIVE ASPECTS. MAKE A LIST OF THINGS YOU LOVE – AND NEVER COMPLAIN ABOUT ANYTHING. AND AS YOU USE THOSE THINGS THAT SHINE BRIGHT AND MAKE YOU FEEL GOOD, AS YOUR EXCUSE TO GIVE YOUR ATTENTION AND BE WHO-YOU-ARE, YOU WILL TUNE TO WHO-YOU-ARE, AND THE WHOLE WORLD WILL BEGIN TO TRANSFORM BEFORE YOUR EYES. IT IS NOT YOUR JOB TO TRANSFORM THE WORLD FOR OTHERS – BUT IT IS YOUR JOB TO TRANSFORM IT FOR YOU."

-ABRAHAM

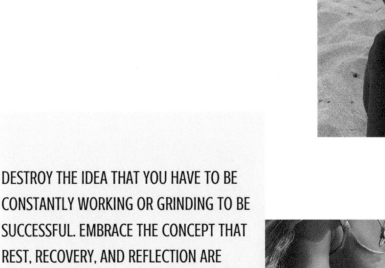

DESTROY THE IDEA THAT YOU HAVE TO BE CONSTANTLY WORKING OR GRINDING TO BE SUCCESSFUL. EMBRACE THE CONCEPT THAT REST, RECOVERY, AND REFLECTION ARE ESSENTIAL PARTS OF THE PROGRESS TOWARD A SUCCESSFUL, HAPPY LIFE.

-KOMPAK

Find out what makes you kinder, what opens you up and brings out the most loving, generous, and unafraid version of you, and go after those things as if nothing else matters.

-George Saunders

**TALKING ABOUT OUR PROBLEMS IS OUR GREATEST ADDICTION. BREAK THE HABIT. TALK ABOUT YOUR JOYS. -RITA SCHIANO**

I'M DANCING AND PUTTING THINGS ON HANGERS. I AM SO GRATEFUL TO BE CLEANING MY ROOM WITH THE WINDOWS OPEN.

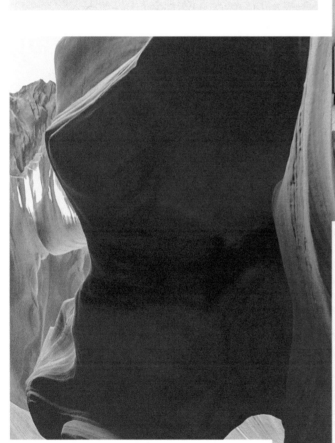

DO WHAT MAKES YOU NERVOUS.
ASK FOR RIDICULOUS THINGS,
AND EXPECT THEM.
HAVE AWKWARD CONVERSATIONS.
IT'S TIME TO CHASE YOUR DREAMS,
AND START LIVING THE LIFE YOU
WANT.

Just one small positive thought in the morning can change your whole day.
-Dalai Lama

BELIEVE IN IT UNTIL IT MANIFESTS FOR YOU. DON'T OVERTHINK HOW IT WILL HAPPEN. DON'T WORRY ABOUT WHEN IT WILL HAPPEN. JUST BELIEVE IN IT. BELIEVE IN YOURSELF.

-IDIL AHMED

WHAT DO YOU LOVE ABOUT THIS PRESENT MOMENT?

Make your morning routine a priority. Stretch your body. Practice gratitude. Moisturize your skin. Pick out a beautiful perfume. Make breakfast for yourself. Take your vitamins. Drink water. Do well by yourself.

-GirlsBuildingEmpires

**"IT'S NOT HARD. YOU HAVE JUST NEVER DONE IT BEFORE. SEE THE DIFFERENCE. EMBRACE YOUR CURIOSITY. SHIFT YOUR PERSPECTIVE."**

**DOCUMENT THE MOMENTS YOU FEEL MOST IN LOVE WITH YOURSELF – WHAT YOU'RE WEARING. WHO YOU ARE AROUND. WHAT YOU ARE DOING. RECREATE AND REPEAT.**

**-WARSAN SHIRE**

It's the small things.

How you spend your mornings. How you talk to yourself. What you read. What you watch. Who you share your energy with. Who has access to you.

That will change your life.

-Michael Tonge

DETOX YOUR ENTIRE LIFE.
CLEAN YOUR BODY, MIND, AND SOUL.
YOUR HOUSE, YOUR CAR, YOUR PHONE.
GET EVERYTHING IN ALIGNMENT.

TRAIN YOUR MIND TO SEE THE GOOD
IN EVERYTHING.

POSITIVITY IS A CHOICE.

THE HAPPINESS OF YOUR LIFE
DEPENDS ON THE QUALITY OF YOUR
THOUGHTS.

-MARCUS AURELIUS ❤

I JUST LOVE THE THOUGHT THAT GREAT THINGS ARE COMING. NO MATTER WHAT YOU'RE CURRENTLY GOING THROUGH, THERE'S SO MUCH TO LOOK FORWARD TO.

Decrease your workload by 30% and increase your fun load by 30% and you will increase your revenues by 100%. And you will increase your productivity by 10,000% (if there could be such a percentage). More fun, less struggle - and more results on all fronts.
-Abraham Hicks

Drive with the windows down.
Live Louder.
Bake your favorite cake.
Take time for yourself.
Keep going.
Be amazing.
Make yourself proud

-Frachella

This chapter feels really good.

"BE A CURATOR OF YOUR LIFE.
SLOWLY CUT THINGS OUT UNTIL
YOU'RE LEFT WITH WHAT YOU
LOVE, WITH WHAT'S NECESSARY
WITH WHAT MAKES YOU HAPPY."

—LEO BABAUTA

BE YOUR BEST FRIEND. BE
YOUR GYM PARTNER. BE
YOUR COFFEE BUDDY. BE
EVERYTHING FOR YOURSELF
RATHER THAN BEING
EVERYTHING FOR SOMEONE
ELSE.

-UNKOWN

GET READY TO LEVEL UP:

MENTALLY

EMOTIONALLY

FINANCIALLY

SPIRITUALLY

ENERGETICALLY

- IT'S ALL COMING

What's stopping you?

"DON'T WASTE YOUR TIME CHASING BUTTERFLIES. MEND YOUR GARDEN, AND THE BUTTERFLIES WILL COME."
-MARIO QUINTANA

If your body is telling you to avoid certain foods and eat more veggies, do it. If your gut is saying to stay away from certain people and get closer to others, do it. If your heart is telling you to quit that job, start that project, take a break, travel, do it. Your higher self knows what is best for you, so don't ignore it.

WHAT A WONDERFUL LIFE THIS IS

I HOPE THERE ARE DAYS WHEN YOUR
COFFEE TASTES LIKE MAGIC, YOUR
PLAYLIST MAKES YOU DANCE,
STRANGERS MAKE YOU SMILE, AND
THE NIGHT SKY TOUCHES YOUR SOUL.
I HOPE THERE ARE DAYS WHEN YOU
FALL IN LOVE WITH BEING ALIVE.

-Brooke Hampton

"THE UNIVERSE IS ALWAYS
SPEAKING TO US... SENDING
US LITTLE MESSAGES,
CAUSING COINCIDENCES
AND SERENDIPITIES,
REMINDING US TO STOP, TO
LOOK AROUND, TO BELIEVE
IN SOMETHING ELSE,
SOMETHING MORE."

YOU HAVE THE POTENTIAL TO
MAKE BEAUTIFUL THINGS.

YES, YOU

Rise and shine, sweet girl.
This is your moment.

-Stephanie May Wilson

FOR MORE MOOD BOOKS VISIT
WWW.ELEVEN22MOOD.COM

♥ELEVEN22
mood

Printed in the United States
by Baker & Taylor Publisher Services